IMAGES
of England

HITCHIN

IMAGES
of England

HITCHIN

Simon Walker

TEMPUS

Bancroft, looking north, *c.* 1870. This area was primarily residential, so market day must have been a nightmare – cattle and sheep were traded directly in front of these substantial homes.

Frontispiece: Walter Stubley's advertisement from *The Hitchin Directory* of 1929, published by Paternoster and Hales. This was the fifty-eighth year of the publication.

First published 2003

Tempus Publishing Limited
The Mill, Brimscombe Port,
Stroud, Gloucestershire, GL5 2QG

British Library Cataloguing in Publication Data.
A catalogue record for this book is available from the British Library.

ISBN 0 7524 2937 X

Typesetting and origination by Tempus Publishing Limited
Printed in Great Britain by Midway Colour Print, Wiltshire

Contents

Acknowledgements

It is both difficult and dangerous to try and rank by importance the help given in the production of a book. True to form, I will take the easy way out and opt for alphabetical order. Almost without exception people have been generous with their time and their treasured photographs. I owe them a debt of gratitude. All those listed below have provided either pictures or assistance in some other way.

I have especially to thank Scilla Douglas, for her proof-reading and advice.

My thanks go to Mr F. Andrews, Chris Ashton, Margaret and Ethel Brinklow, the late Mr D.G. Burton, David Chalkley, David Cole, Jimmy Dawson, Scilla Douglas, David Fyfe, Pat Gadd-Thurstance, Mark Gimson, P. Gould, Dudley Hall, Chris Hubbard, Laurie Hughes, Pauline Humphries, David Jones, Tony Leone, Pansy Mitchell, Bob Prebble, Mary Swain, Pat Thornhill, Roger and Pat Wallace, Sidney and Margaret Watson, Derek Wheeler and Terry Wilson.

I should also like to acknowledge the research put into the history of Hitchin by the many writers of books about the town, especially Denis Dolan, Joyce Donald, Scilla Douglas, Richard Fielding, Alan Fleck, Tony Foster, Sue Fitzpatrick, Pat Gadd-Thurstance, Pauline Humphries, Reginald Hine, Bridget Howlett, Alan Millard, Helen Parker, Ron Pigram, Barry West and Richard Whitmore.

I hope I have not forgotten anyone. If I have, I apologise unreservedly.

Introduction

This book is a collection of photographs, many of them previously unpublished, of the streets, buildings and people of Hitchin in the nineteenth and twentieth centuries. It is not a complete history, because it depends upon the pictures that are available. It is perhaps more like a lucky dip.

I have deliberately excluded many of the better-known pictures, and used a few that are of less than perfect quality. If a picture is sufficiently interesting I have included it nonetheless. There are a few old favourites that I could not omit, either because they have not appeared for some time or because they are just too good to leave out.

Hitchin is a market town in North Hertfordshire, within two miles of the Bedfordshire border. The town retains many of its older buildings, though some have, sadly, been lost to what is euphemistically termed 'development'. The Angel Vaults, the Croft and other structures from the fourteenth century lasted for 500 years, only to fall prey to commercialism.

It should not be thought that demolition is a new process in Hitchin, though in previous centuries the size of the town allowed for expansion rather than demolition and rebuilding; perhaps too a lack of funds to enable rebuilding has saved some of our heritage. But it is true that the greater part of the damage occurred in the twentieth century. Fortunately, this was also the age of the camera, and Hitchin was particularly well served by early exponents of the art, such as the Thomas Latchmores, father and son, and Henry Moulden. Amateur photographers too played an important role in recording the town's history.

The region of North Hertfordshire has been settled for thousands of years. Stone implements have been found that suggest a prehistoric settlement; pottery from the Bronze Age and tools and weapons from the Iron Age have also come to light. There have been finds from the Roman period and a villa was excavated between Purwell and Wymondley in the late nineteenth century by William Ransom. Recent excavations have revealed signs of Saxon activity, with a palisade running parallel to and east of Queen Street. It was in about AD 600 that the town got its name, from a Saxon tribe, the Hicce. King Offa had an interest in the town, and established a religious foundation here in AD 792. By the time of the Norman Conquest Hitchin was a royal manor. Over the next 900 years Hitchin grew, its wealth from the wool trade resulting in St Mary's church, a massive building for a small town.

In the nineteenth and twentieth centuries the Tuesday market drew traders from the surrounding villages and, following the coming of the railway in 1850, from further afield. Cattle and livestock were bought and sold in Bancroft, and later in Paynes Park, whilst general market goods were traded in the Market Place. Straw plait for the Luton hat industry formed a significant commodity, and with other commerce, including grain, brought pressure for a second market day on Saturdays. The cattle and livestock markets are now gone, but Hitchin still has a general market, one of the most vibrant in south-east England.

For many years the market was held in the Market Place, but after the Second World War it moved to St Mary's Square. In 1971 it moved again, to the area immediately south of Biggin Lane. This is the site it occupies at present, though it has spilled out along the River Hiz in St Mary's Square.

The old part of Hitchin runs approximately north to south: the Priory is to the south and Bancroft (once Silver Street) to the north. The medieval town was on this alignment, from Tilehouse Street to Bancroft. Originally the market stalls were temporary, but as time went by traders made them permanent, resulting in the town layout we see today. Sun Street, Bucklersbury, the Market Place, the High Street and the west side of the churchyard were built up by this infill, resulting in a classic market town shape. Incidentally, an interesting feature of the Market Place is that many of the buildings surrounding it have cellars reaching far beyond their above ground boundaries – an ideal way to get hold of extra storage space.

In the nineteenth century there was substantial growth in the town, predominantly to the north towards the station. The twentieth century saw further development, extending the urban area in all directions except to the south west. As well as piecemeal development, whole estates were built in Westmill, Walsworth, Purwell and the Oakfield area. To the north the Wilbury Way industrial estate expanded towards the Roman Icknield Way.

Now, in the early years of the twenty-first century, the emphasis is on brownfield sites within the existing boundaries of the town. This trend brings special challenges in the preservation of the town's archaeology and character.

On a lighter note, if I seem to concentrate heavily on public houses it is because ,firstly, they are frequently photographed as local focal points; and secondly, there were once a lot of them! The numbers have now declined to below thirty, but there was once twice that, and serving a much smaller population.

I hope that readers who live in Hitchin will find something here to interest them; and I hope that those residing elsewhere will be encouraged to visit the town. Despite the developers' best efforts it retains much of its old-world charm, as well as some outstanding features of historical importance.

Simon Walker

One

Transport

A tricycle outside the Hermitage in Bancroft, c. 1880. The manufacturer was the Quadrant Tricycle Company, of Sheepcote Street, Birmingham, who made high-quality, if somewhat complex, machines. It is chain driven, and has a rather elaborate steering mechanism. The company also made tandem tricycles. The significance of the chair held by the young onlooker is a mystery.

Members of the Blue Cross Temperance Cycle Club pose at the Hare and Hounds in Old Warden around 1890. Cycling was a popular sport in the last quarter of the nineteenth century, and this group includes a penny-farthing and a tricycle as well as machines of a more orthodox design. As we shall see later, more than one hotel in Hitchin catered specifically for touring cyclists. The woman on the right must have turned her head as the photograph was taken.

A Foden steam wagon outside the Lucas brewery on the corner of Sun and Bridge Streets in about 1910. The internal combustion engine did not replace steam as a motive force for many years, and vehicles like this one were once quite common. The major disadvantage was the time taken to gain a head of steam, though disposal of the ashes from the fire could also be a nuisance.

Bridge Street, looking towards Sun Street, c. 1910. The signs indicate that the age of the motorcar had arrived. Slater Batty & Co. advertise, on the left, 'Shell motor spirit' and 'Pratt's motor spirit', along with 'Vacuum motor car oils'. On the other side of the road is their mechanical, electrical and motor car repair works. There is a sign recommending Michelin tyres. The inner man is catered for too: on the left, the Royal Oak Inn, and on the right an establishment provides 'Hot Dinners Daily. Tea, Coffee, Cocoa. Cycles Stored'. The horse was, however, to remain a source of pulling power until after the Second World War.

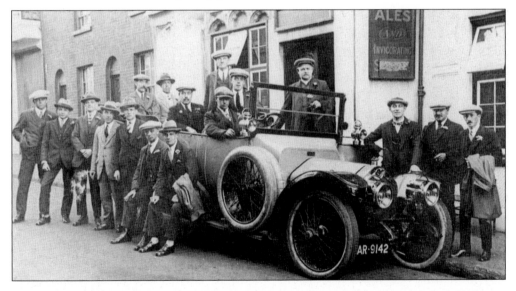

A fine motor car, believed to be a Crossley, stands outside the Coopers' Arms in Tilehouse Street. The vehicle has acetylene headlamps and oil sidelights, suggesting a date of around 1910. It has Rudge Whitworth quick-release wheels, and carries two spares. The registration number, AR 9142, is a Hertfordshire number dating from 1919 or 1920. It is possible that the car was requisitioned during the First World War and later re-registered on its release from service.

After the Second World War there was a resurgence in private motoring, and motorcycles were popular. This AJS machine is being ridden by Peter Wells in 1952; his sister, Pansy, is the passenger. The headgear – a pair of goggles – was quite normal at the time. Before the war AJS had been taken over by Matchless to form Associated Motor Cycles. The photograph was taken in West Hill.

A steamroller in Brand Street in about 1935. These machines were an essential part of road maintenance. The registration is UR 9678, and the prancing horse emblem indicates that this one was made by the Aveling company. These vehicles weighed up to ten tons.

Hitchin station, before it was rebuilt in 1910, when a large canopy designed to keep travellers dry when disembarking from their vehicles was added, only to be demolished again at the end of 1974. The railway came to Hitchin in 1850 in the form of the Great Northern Railway and, as elsewhere in the country, ruined the coaching industry wherever the two competed. The train was more comfortable, cheaper and quicker than a coach.

Hitchin station, the northbound platform, in the 1880s. In the background a sign reads, 'Passengers are earnestly requested to cross the railway by the bridge'. Apart from books and newspapers, the kiosk also sold Hitchin lavender water.

A Sturrock 2-2-2 engine, built by Kitsons for the Great Northern Railway in Hitchin locomotive yard. It was taken on stock in May 1860. The 'A' was added to its number in 1886. From 1887 to its withdrawal from service in 1897, this engine was stationed at Hitchin, and it is from this decade that this photograph dates. Pulling twelve coaches, 70mph could be achieved by these locomotives. During the Second World War the Special Operations Executive trained agents how to blow up trains in these sidings at Hitchin.

This biplane, said to be at the Roman Camp, Wilbury Hills, has so far remained unidentified. According to the caption it is a military aircraft. If so it looks like an early one – it may be a civilian machine requisitioned by the forces at the start of the war in August 1914. The engine seems to be of rotary design.

Two
Business and Industry

John Walker outside his butcher's shop at No. 26 Queen Street in 1887. Above the door is a flag, suggesting that this carefully posed picture was taken on the occasion of Queen Victoria's Golden Jubilee in that year. The objects hanging on the left-hand-side of the awning are bullock's hearts. Oxtails hang from the right of the awning. This print was made over a hundred years ago, and has unfortunately deteriorated somewhat.

W.B. Moss's first shop in Bancroft, towards the north end of the street. Next door was W. Jelly's tinware shop. Both buildings were demolished in the late nineteenth century. A new police station was built to replace the old Bridewell that stood a little further north, on the other side of the road. The new station opened in 1885 and included quarters for the policemen, as well as the magistrates' court. This picture is believed to date from the 1870s.

Allingham's butchers is one of the few traditional butchers remaining in Hitchin. This advertisement dates from 1929, and offers a higher level of service than one might expect today. In common with several other premises in the Market Place, Allinghams has a cellar that extends well beyond the shop frontage. It comes in very useful for storage, especially during the Christmas period.

Premises at No. 10 Bancroft, opposite Hermitage Road, belonging to A. Waters & Sons, removers, established in 1887. Waters used the site until it was cleared to make way for what was then Safeway's supermarket. A fine Georgian structure, its loss was greatly mourned at the time.

One of Waters' competitors for domestic removals was J. Deamer & Son of Paynes Park, who described themselves as the 'premier North Herts removers'.

W.B. Moss & Sons demolished their old premises at Moss's Corner (once the Troopers' Arms) in 1899. When this advertisement appeared in 1902, the new shop on the site had already opened. There were Moss branches in Baldock, Fenny Stratford, Otley, Ripon and, later, Shefford.

18

THIS Store was built with bricks and mortar in nine months, but it has taken a quarter of a century to build up this business to its present dimensions—the largest in the district.

and Sons, —

ᴛ, HITCHIN.

1902.

eed of a Household Store—a Store capable of supplying its country customers with
hich covers, as with a network, the whole countryside, supplying its customers at
ind this store was built   Wiseacres shook their heads and said it could never be a
m to-day to carry all the goods our business demands, and with pardonable pride we

W.E. Osborne's 'hygienic bakery' in Orchard Road, Walsworth. The bearded gentleman is Mr Osborne, the proprietor. The cart emerging from the side passage delivered bread in the area. The bakery ovens were sometimes used to roast over-large joints of meat for locals at Christmas. This photograph dates from around 1920.

Osborne's bakery soon decided that a van was necessary to the business, and invested in this Model T Ford, beside which stands Tom Osborne, the owner's son. The bakery was at this time still described as hygienic, but now its produce is 'machine made'.

An elevator belonging to Percy Webb, implement agent and agricultural engineer of No. 17 Bridge Street, being drawn by two magnificent draft horses. His premises were next to the river, on the south side of the road. This picture was taken in Bedford Road, outside the hospital. The picture is difficult to date, but is probably from around 1925. 'Neddy' Bradford is in the middle of the picture; the others are unidentified.

Munt's, in the High Street, as the shop appeared in an advertisement of 1935. There was also a branch in Letchworth. Apart from bicycles and baby carriages, the shop sold all sorts of toys, including cap guns and trains for boys and dolls for girls. The passageway to the left of the shop leads into the churchyard.

G.C. Flanders

Carriage and

Motor Car

Builder,

MARKET

SQUARE,

HITCHIN.

G.C. Flanders, of the Market Place, advertised in 1902 as 'Carriage and Motor Car Builder'. The company also dealt in cycles and athletic goods. The car on the right is probably a Daimler, but it is difficult to be certain.

Bullard's basket shop in the churchyard. The figure on the left is thought to be James Bullard, who died in 1913, the last of several generations of basket makers. This picture must date from before 1899 because part of the Trooper's Arms, demolished that year, is visible in the background (centre). To the right is Tomlin's fruitier and greengrocer. Bullard offered 'English and Foreign Baskets'. He also had a stall at the Tuesday market, near what is now the old arcade.

This rare picture shows Paternoster & Hales' book folding and sewing department in the late nineteenth century. The Paternoster family had been in Hitchin for many years when the business went into partnership with Charles Hales in the 1870s. The company occupied several premises, including the south-west corner of the Market Place and the Printing Office in Sun Street. In addition to printing, for one guinea a year one could join their circulating library. Books could be borrowed at 2d per volume.

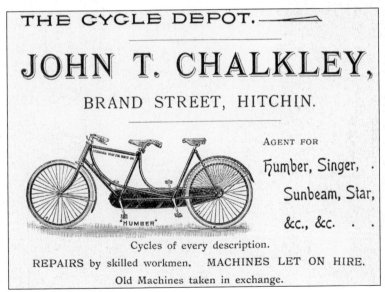

Advertisement for John Chalkley's Cycle Depot from an almanac of 1899. The tandem is a Humber, and the crossbar is marked 'detachable stay for gents use'. Three years later the business had become the 'Cycle and Motor Works', and its range extended to include Excelsior motorcycles and the 'celebrated noiseless Locomobile steam car'. Chalkley modestly advertised his cycles as being the same as those ridden by 'Their Majesties Edward VII and the Kings of Italy, Belgium and Greece'.

Harding's wholesale newsagent's shop in Tilehouse Street in the 1930s. The woman in the picture is believed to be Mrs Harding. Once the Three Tuns public house, by the 1950s the building had become semi-derelict, and only the hallway and front room were in use. It was restored to a high standard in the early 1980s.

Wells' garage in West Hill between the wars. Built by Frank 'Bert' Wells and his father in 1925, the workshop and pumps are still there today. The site has been designated by North Hertfordshire District Council as being of local historic interest. Vehicles in this picture include two Talbots, a Rover 12hp and an Oldsmobile. An inventor and engineer, Bert Wells also built the bungalow behind the workshop and generated his own electricity.

Innes and Kings of Walsworth Road in 1914. Bert Wells is machining shells for the British Expeditionary Force. The firm originally made agricultural machinery, but they also made castings, and drain covers with their name on them can still be seen in the town. The business moved to Stevenage in 1952. Soon after this picture was taken, Bert Wells was sent to France, where the following year he came across one of the shells he had made himself.

Bowman's Mill, at the junction of Walsworth Road and Nightingale Road, was built in 1901 as a steam mill. The site was selected for its proximity to the railway; in fact it was known as 'Station Mill.' By 1914 Bowmans were milling flour at Hitchin, Astwick and Ickleford, and animal feed at Hyde Mill and West Mill, which were still water powered. Station Mill was damaged by fire in 1947, caused by that nightmare of millers everywhere, the overheated bearing.

A Bowman's flour bag from 1966. For many years Bowman's flour was available in local shops, but eventually the company decided that it could not compete in the retail market place with the big manufacturers, and decided to concentrate on bulk sales to the catering industry.

Cadwell lime works, *c.* 1910. On a map of 1880 they are shown as the Greystone lime works. This pit was formed by the removal of chalk for the limekilns. From the pit it was carried in horse-drawn wagons to the kilns for burning. The lime produced was spread on the fields as a soil improver, used in mortar and in sewage purifiers. It was also the chief constituent of lime wash. Lime burning often went hand in hand with brick making, as both employed similar technologies.

Feeding the limekilns. The chalk had to be heated for about seventy hours before the process was complete. There were more lime works just to the south of Hitchin station, by the chalk cliffs that are a feature of the area. They were owned by Alfred Ransom, who lived in Benslow, and who built a tunnel at the end of his estate to allow easy access to his works below.

A Local Industry

PERKS' LAVENDER

PERKS EXTRACT OF ENGLISH LAVENDER FLOWERS

PERKS MOUNT PLEASANT LAVENDER FIELD.

PERKS' LAVENDER WATER

is prepared from Lavender grown in our own fields and distilled in Hitchin. Other fragrant and refreshing specialities include Talcum Powder, Bath Salts, Smelling Salts, Cold Cream and Lavender Sachets

PERKS AND LLEWELLYN

Chemists and Lavender Cultivators

HIGH STREET   HITCHIN

An advertisement for Perks & Llewellyn from 1952. Perks & Llewellyn produced a range of toiletries based on lavender, grown locally in fields to the west of the town. Their chemists' shop in the High Street closed in 1961, but many of the fittings were saved and are on display in Hitchin Museum as a reconstruction of a chemist's shop. The house in the centre of this advertisement has, sadly, been demolished.

Lavender gathering, c. 1955. Mrs Vicki Bryder and Miss Isobel French harvest the crop by hand. Perks & Llewellyn were not the only lavender distillers in Hitchin – both Wm. Ransom & Son and Martins produced lavender oil and water. Amongst the other plants Ransom's experimented with was the wonderfully named 'spitting cucumber', more commonly found in the Mediterranean.

Opposite below: The Post Office depot in King's Road in 1938. In 1928 the Post Office opened its sorting office on the site, and Post Office Telephones shared the premises. The plot is now private housing. Amongst the vehicles are vans and trucks made by Albion, Austin and Morris. Fourth from the left in the front row is lineman Walter Prebble. Also in the picture are Bill Munroe, Herbert Carr, Arthur Darkin and Alfred Spriggs, who was in charge of the motorcycle and sidecar.

P.H. Barker & Son joinery works on the corner of Bancroft and Hermitage Road in the late nineteenth century. The fifteenth-century hall they occupied, with its seventeenth-century gables, was demolished in 1958, and the business moved to Cadwell Lane. When box trees on the east side of Bancroft were felled in 1919, Barker's used some of the timber to make a gavel and block, which can be seen in Hitchin Museum.

Cadwell, the gas conversion works in 1971. The plant converted butane and 'raw' gas to town gas, but was made obsolete by the move to natural gas. It was in use for only eleven years. During its lifetime it appeared in several films and advertisements, including one for Martini. Demolition began in 1974.

The Letchworth Hill Laundry in Hampden Road. The business was opened by Mr William Fyfe in June 1938, but when the Second World War began the premises were taken over by the Civil Defence, and were used for gas mask distribution. After the war normal business resumed, and the company continues its laundry service on the same site today. The van on the right is a Bedford.

Harkness Rose Gardens were opened in the 1890s by R. Harkness, and have had a reputation for excellence ever since. The company has won numerous awards, including, in 1995, their fifteenth consecutive gold medal at the Chelsea Flower Show. The business has been recognized in the naming of the Rosehill estate, which includes Harkness Way.

Harkness Rose Gardens in the 1940s, between Stotfold Road and the A505 (Cambridge Road). Percy Pettengell is driving the Farmall tractor; the men hoeing behind him are Arthur Street, Arthur Aldridge and Ernest Richards.

Highover Farm, c. 1930. This and the following photograph depict a traction engine gang. The gang were contracted out to work on various farms, as the cost of the equipment was too high for all but the largest farms. The men worked from the van shown here. Mr A.W. Edwards, whose name appears on the van, farmed at Highover between 1902 and the early 1930s, though whether he owned the equipment is unknown.

Highover Farm; the engine is a Fowler ploughing engine, though in this picture it seems to be clearing brushwood, perhaps from a hedgerow. Normally the cable from the drum beneath the body of the machine pulled the plough from one side of the field to the other, via a horizontal wheel or a second engine. Steam ploughing was twenty times as fast as horse ploughing.

Three
Buildings

The Priory, viewed from what is now the rear, though this was for many years the main entrance of the building. A Carmelite priory was established here in 1317, but it was seized and sold by agents of Henry VIII in 1539. The buildings we see today were built by John Radcliffe in about 1775; very little remains of the original buildings. There were flowerbeds to the left and right that were at one time planted according to a plan by Gertrude Jekyll.

The Biggin, before its renovation in 1960. The Biggin was built as a priory, founded in 1361 by the Gilbertine order. It has been largely rebuilt, but retains much of its charm. Like the Priory, it was sold by agents of Henry VIII. Contrary to popular belief, there is no evidence to suggest that the Biggin housed nuns, nor to corroborate the story that a tunnel connects it to the Priory, used by the Carmelite brothers for illicit night trysts with their Gilbertine sisters.

The interior of the Biggin, c. 1905. On the right are the wooden columns of the 'Tuscan' colonnade, an unusual feature of the courtyard. When this picture was taken the building was an almshouse, with a communal water pump in the courtyard. It has also served as a school in its chequered career.

The old town hall (right) in Brand Street dates from 1840, and is now used as council offices. Next door is the Mechanics' Institute and Library, which opened in 1861. The creation of the Institute in 1835 was an important step in the improvement in education; twenty-six years on, the building provided it with a home. The Institute put on lectures from time to time, usually given by prominent local citizens.

The new town hall, *c.* 1905. This was built on the site of W. Jelly's workshop by Fosters, a firm of local builders, at a cost of £7,300. The new building was opened on 18 March 1901 by Mrs Hudson, wife of the local MP. To the right of the entrance a small girl stands by a sign reading 'The Sign of the Cross', with a date of Tuesday 18 July.

The interior of the Corn Exchange, built in 1853. This lithograph may be a preliminary design; the iron roof supports in the actual building are arched. The design was by William Beck, a local architect, and was submitted free of charge as a prestige project. It was the coming of the railway that gave impetus to the venture, but the Exchange was not a great success. The building has also served as a roller-skating rink and an indoor market. It is now a bar.

Ransom's entrance in Bancroft, mid-twentieth century. It is a fine half-timbered building and has changed very little in a hundred years. Above the window in the right-hand gable is a firemark for the Phoenix Assurance Company. The business was started by William Ransom in 1846. Like Perks & Llewellyn, Ransom distilled lavender, but he went further – he was a pharmaceutical chemist. The company is still active in the pharmaceutical industry today.

Hitchin Library and Museum in the 1940s. The house was called Charnwood, and dates from 1825. It was once a private residence, but in 1936 Hubert and Wallace Moss bought it for the town, and after alterations it became the library in 1938. From 1941 the museum occupied the first floor. A substantial extension was added in the 1960s, into which the library moved, leaving the original building for the museum.

The Croft in Bancroft, centre right, in the late nineteenth century. The building that stands on the spot today is a reproduction. The original was thought to be a woolstapler's hall, and dated from the early fourteenth century, though there were considerable alterations in the seventeenth and nineteenth centuries. The Croft was demolished in 1964/65 in order that more practical shop accommodation might be provided. At least some attempt was made when rebuilding to reproduce the original, sadly not always the case.

The German Hospital off Benslow Lane was built in 1908 as a convalescent home for the German community in London. Princess Louise Augusta of Schleswig-Holstein laid the foundation stone. The military took the building over during the First World War and it became a hospital for the treatment of Allied troops, the irony of which cannot have been lost on the military planners. Today it is the private Pinehill Hospital.

West Mill on the River Oughton, date unknown. The mill gave its name to the estate that was built, at least in part, to accommodate those displaced by the slum clearance of the Queen Street area. The original buildings dated from the early seventeenth century but were rebuilt in the 1700s. The water in the foreground is the millpond. Unfortunately most of the mill was destroyed in a fire in 1961.

Purwell Mill on the River Purwell, as it appeared in 1949; it is very little changed today. The site has been a mill for centuries – John Millere was the tenant in 1470. A few years ago the current owner, Don Smith, established that his kitchen was built above the mill-race, and removed part of the floor to investigate. He discovered that when the mill had been renovated the contractors had not removed the mill-wheel but cut it off and floored over it. It remains there to this day.

Thatched cottage in Wymondley Road, Ninesprings, in the early 1950s. It had no electricity, and water had to be carried in buckets from the nearby watercress beds. Though apparently ramshackle, it was still occupied when this photograph was taken. It has now been demolished.

Nutleigh Grove, at the corner of Redhill Road and Bedford Road. A fine Victorian building, during the Second World War it was battalion headquarters to the Royal Engineers, after which it was divided into flats. In the 1960s it fell into disrepair and was demolished to make way for the Angel's Reply public house. The name is retained in Nutleigh Grove, a cul-de-sac off Redhill Road, built in 1932.

The Tollgate Cottage, on the south side of the junction of Bedford Road and Westmill Lane. It was built as a tollhouse in 1757 for the Hitchin, Shefford and Bedford Turnpike Trust. Travellers paid a fee to use the road, which was maintained by the Trust. The fee depended upon the type of traffic: a wagon or coach paid more than a pedestrian. The building was demolished when the Bedford Road was widened and the junction improved.

Four
Streetscapes

Tilehouse Street, looking west, in about 1900. On the left is the Three Tuns; on the other side of the road the premises with the awnings are home to Taylor's Hygienic Bakery, with their Baily-Baker hot-air oven. Apart from the railings on the left, and modern street lighting, very little has changed in the last 100 years.

Charlton Road (now known as Wratten Road East), looking towards Tilehouse Street. These rather dilapidated buildings are the Wratten Maltings. For some time the site was used as a storage depot by Fosters, a firm of local builders, before making way for bank offices in the 1960s. The name 'Wratten' is believed to come from the Anglo-Saxon *wrœtt*, meaning crosswort (*cruciata laevipes*), and *tun*, meaning farm or place. Hence, the place where the crosswort grows.

Bridge Street, looking east from the junction with Sun Street, *c.* 1914. On the left is the Lucas Brewery, founded in 1709. The business was bought out by J.W. Green Ltd of Luton in 1920, who closed the brewery just three years later. The buildings lasted until 1963, when they were demolished. On the right, just before the bridge for which Bridge Street is named, is the Plough Inn. C.R. Burrows, on the right, advertised as an 'upholsterer, cabinet maker and decorator', but also sold household goods, including china and glass.

Bridge Street, looking west, early in the twentieth century. On the left is the parapet of the bridge, dating from 1784. In earlier days there was a ford here across the River Hiz. The bridge was recently rebuilt to comply with weight requirements for heavy vehicles. Next to it is the Plough. Mr H. Crawley's butchers comes next. The entrance to Sun Street is just out of shot on the right.

The Triangle, viewed from Park Street, c. 1890. At the junction of Bridge Street, Park Street and Queen Street, this intersection was once known as Bull Corner; it has been suggested that the barbaric sport of bull-baiting once took place there. Queen Street, on the right, was once called Dead Street, allegedly after all its inhabitants perished in the plague.

The same view, c. 1960. Buildings to the right of the Hill View Hotel, which was run by A.G. Bottoms, have gone, as have the houses on the left. Soon after this photograph was taken the hotel itself gave way to Saunders Garage (now a pine shop and fitness centre). The large concrete block on the left is thought to be a roadblock – a remnant from the Second World War. Just visible to the right of the picture is the Hitchin British Schools.

Park Street, looking north, c. 1890. Just out of sight around the bend is the Triangle. The wall to the left, looking much as it does today, dates from around 1800, and encloses the Priory Park. The turn in the wall locates the position of the photographer exactly. The buildings on the right were 'Fordham's Blacksmith and Beer Retailer'. This side of the road is now much changed; most of the houses are gone. On the far right, the sandy bank is shored up with timber, and not without good cause. Only a few years ago, part of the bank and a wall a little further down the road collapsed onto a Range Rover, writing the vehicle off.

Park Street and Hitchin Hill, *c.* 1900. The road once followed the same level as the path upon which the children are congregated. This caused serious problems for horse-drawn traffic, especially coming downhill, as there was a tight bend at the bottom. In 1806 the Welwyn Turnpike Trust cut through the hill from the Three Moorhens to Standhill Road, levelling out the gradient.

Park Street and Hitchin Hill a few years later, and civilization has stamped itself onto the landscape. The rough path has given way to concrete steps and railings fence off what must have been a child's delight. The road to the right ran to Gosmore, but now goes no further than the Three Moorhens.

Chapman's Yard, late nineteenth century. The yard ran from Queen Street to the Hiz. It is believed to have been named after William Chapman, keeper of the Peahen public house. Behind the attractive frontage lay slum housing. In early 1849 a government health inspector, William Ranger, reported that there were seventeen houses with a total of ninety occupants; the only two privies discharged directly into the river. The nearby Hewitts Yard had only three privies for 129 people. The slums were cleared in the 1920s and the inhabitants moved to healthier accommodation.

Sun Street, looking towards the Market Place, c. 1925. The Sun Hotel, after which the street is named, is on the right. Hitchin's magistrates met in this important coaching inn for many years. Beyond the Sun is the Angel Vaults, another important inn – indeed, the road was once called Angel Street. Immediately opposite the Sun is Paternoster & Hales' Printing Office.

Sun Street, and an unusual view of the courtyard behind Paternoster & Hales' Printing Office during drainage work. Of particular interest is the colonnaded walkway beneath the jetty of the weatherboard building. Drainage was always a problem in the Sun Street/Bridge Street area, with floods of both water and sewage, even after the installation of drains in the 1850s.

The Market Place looking south, *c.* 1880. The buildings are little changed. Gatward jewellers, the oldest family jewellers in the county, are still in business, and have expanded to take over the premises of Whaley's hairdressers next door. Shilcocks' gothic building, with it's turret, continues to puzzle visitors to the town. Melia & Co. was a grocery chain, though their heart seems to have been in tea. On the right-hand corner is Charles Hales' Bookbinding and Printing Works.

Bucklersbury, looking towards the Market Place, before 1904. The Red Hart is the first pub on the left; it was recently damaged by fire, but fortunately not badly. The George is next, named after George Washington, not one of the royal Georges – Washington's secretary, the Revd William Gordon, was a Hitchin man. The last building visible on the left side of the road is Brookers, the hardware store that has been trading since the 1870s.

The Market Place, to the south west, in the early years of the twentieth century. Hales now reflects the merger with Paternoster Printers. Freeman Hardy & Willis sold shoes, and invested in the mosaic above the entrance to their shop. The Timothy White Company later moved to the High Street. When they were taken over their branch there became Boots. The signage at this time was quite extravagant.

The Market Place, the north-west section, between 1903 and 1910. The Corn Exchange on the left is now a bar. The site of Logsdon's Restaurant, established in 1820, in 1913 became the Playhouse, a cinema seating 750. It closed in 1937 and Burtons tailoring chain took over the site until the late 1970s. The first floor was, and is, a billiard hall. Gatward's sold everything you needed to furnish your house; the owners were related to Gatward jewellers. John R. Jackson was a 'ladies' and children's outfitter'. Briggs & Company's sign is flamboyant to say the least.

The Market Place, the north-west corner, in the 1890s. A. Lamb's shop occupied the site, soon to become Jackson's (see previous picture), though they sold much the same sort of goods. The site was later taken over by the Midland Bank, now HSBC, whose building was a sympathetic addition to the Market Place. Next door is the post office, which moved to Brand Street in 1904. The letterbox, just below the clock in the window, bears the V.R. monogram for Queen Victoria.

The Market Place, looking north east in the late nineteenth century. Waldock's Bazaar, occupying the buildings left of centre, advertised as 'dyers, cleaners, and feather dressers'. Next comes St Mary's church tower with its Hertfordshire spike steeple. On the right is George Spurr's, drapers, haberdashers, milliners and dressmakers. The shop was in business until the premises were demolished in the 1970s.

The churchyard gates, *c.* 1905. Contrary to local belief, the iron gates were not removed for scrap in 1940. They went in the late 1920s. They had been erected by public subscription after Elizabeth Whitehead's corpse was taken by bodysnatchers in 1828. The cement rendering, intended to give the appearance of stonework, so popular in the nineteenth century, is showing distinct signs of wear on the building to the right. The building to the left was at one time St Mary's vicarage.

The High Street, looking north, in about 1900. Robert Street's jewellers is on the left. Street was a difficult man; when he died in 1908 his obituary read, 'A man of very pronounced opinions, occasionally perhaps there was some excess of warmth in his expression of them, marked as it was by complete candour and fearlessness'. Nonetheless, between 1858 and 1873, when Hitchin was without local government, it was men like Street who stepped in to keep the water and sewage works running. Next door to Street is J.R. Eve & Son, auctioneers and appraisers. Further up is the Black Horse, which closed its doors for the last time in 1958.

High Street, looking south in 1968. The sign with the cross and fish on the left is Macfisheries, a fishmonger chain. On the other side of the street, next to Barclay's Bank, is the original Woolworth building. The Cock Hotel is next, then Perks & Llewellyn, which had closed and was awaiting the demolition team. Woolworth's had acquired the site for expansion. Last of all is the Pipe Shop, which sold a variety of weird and wonderful tobacco products, including snuff.

Moss's Corner, Bancroft, looking south to the High Street. This picture dates from before 1900, as the Trooper's Arms, although owned by Moss, is still standing. In the distance stands the Italianate Corn Exchange in the Market Place. The white building on the right is the Brotherhood House, dating from the fifteenth century. At each end of the roof once stood terracotta figures on horseback, one of which can be seen in Hitchin Museum.

Bancroft, looking south, *c.* 1885. When this picture was taken, much of Bancroft was residential. On the left is the Croft, and two of the granite uprights in front of it still stand. In the centre of the picture stands a knife grinder with his cart. This area was the cattle market for many years, as the road surface seems to reflect.

Bancroft, between Portmill lane and Hermitage Road, *c.* 1929. The destruction of this row of early buildings was a tragedy to Hitchin. Once such historic structures are lost, they are lost forever. The replacements may be practical, but they can hardly be said to be a visual improvement.

Bancroft, looking south towards the High Street. At the centre of the picture is the Hermitage, but there is no trace of Hermitage Road, so the picture must be earlier than 1875. The figure on the right wears a tall top hat, suggesting an early date. The gutter on the right-hand side of the road is more akin to a ditch.

Bancroft: the Hermitage and the entrance to Hermitage Road, probably in the 1880s. When this picture was taken, Hermitage Road was new. Frederic Seebohm, who lived in the Hermitage, centre, gave the land for the new road to improve communications between the town centre and the station. The River Hiz was carried beneath the road through a substantial culvert, with a footpath to one side. The newer entrance and exit are much smaller, giving no clue as to what lies between them.

Bancroft, looking north. The raised pathway is long gone, though its existence is hinted at by the height of the modern pavement. The site of the building on the left became the Regal Cinema, and later, Regal Chambers. The two buildings next door are still there, though No. 53, dating from the late fifteenth, early sixteenth century, has recently been remodelled. At the end of the road, the Adam & Eve is still a pub, though it has been renamed twice and is now called the Phoenix. Putting a date on this picture is particularly difficult, but it is certainly pre-1930.

Skynner's Almshouses, Bancroft, late nineteenth century. This picture shows a cottage that is missing from the previous photograph, so it must be an older view. Skynner's Almshouses on the right were built for John and Ralph Skynner, father and son, in 1666 and 1696 respectively. They were modernized in the 1960s but remain interesting buildings, with contemporary commemorative plaques mounted in the ornate entrances in the front wall.

Bancroft, the north end, in 1937. An atmospheric night view, under sodium street lighting. By this time the pavement on the right of Bancroft had adopted its modern form, and the site of the Regal Cinema had been cleared for development. On the left is Bancroft Recreation Ground, which at this time still had its railings, later sacrificed to the war effort.

Brand Street in the early twentieth century. On the left is Shand's Poultry Mart. On the right, next to the post office of 1904, stood the Methodist chapel from the 1830s, then the Dog public house. Next door but one to the Dog is Hill's Coffee Rooms and Temperance Hotel, who advertised accommodation for 'travellers and cyclists'. This postcard was mailed to a British army corporal stationed in Belgium in 1916.

Hitchin Boys' Grammar School pupils and masters in Brand Street, Founder's Day, 1946. This picture is interesting for the information it provides about the left side of the road, less commonly photographed than the right. Next to Chalkley & Son (cycles) is the Employment Exchange. The 'keep left' sign, with its reflector and black and white painted island, is a relic of the blackout during the Second World War.

Queen Street, between Portmill Lane and Hermitage Road, c. 1950. The lodge at the corner of Whinbush Road is clearly visible in the background. The vehicle is a Land Rover. The road at this time was far narrower then than it is today. The signs at the top of Portmill Lane read 'No Waiting'. Portmill was located on the Hiz, and was bought and demolished by the Local Board of Health in the 1850s, when a sewage system was built in the town. The main run of the system was beneath the bed of the river.

Bancroft and the High Street, c. 1925. Whilst horse-drawn vehicles and bicycles are in evidence, motor vehicles are making their precence felt, including, to the left, an open-topped omnibus.

Bedford Road at the junction with Old Park Road, overlooking Butts Close, in the early twentieth century. The ornate structure on the right is a combined horse trough, drinking fountain and street lamp. The sign below the light points the route to London. A row of trees now runs along this side of the close, and the hedging is gone. Butts Close takes its name from its use as an archery range; for many years practice with the longbow was compulsory for all able-bodied men of the realm. 'Butt' appears in other field names in other towns in England, including Berkhamsted and St Albans.

The junction of Ickleford Road and Nightingale Road before the construction of the Catholic Our Lady Immaculate and St Andrew's church in 1902. The signpost points left to Ickleford, Arlesey and Shefford. The buildings nearest the camera are Fryth Cottages, which date from the early nineteenth century.

Ickleford Road in around 1920. Many of the houses are Victorian; the rest are Edwardian. This was not a planned development, taking place in a somewhat piecemeal manner over half a century or more from the 1860s, the west side (the left in this picture) being completed first. The Victoria public house at the junction with Bancroft, Nightingale Road and Fishponds Road has been licensed since 1865. Somewhat confusingly, the road now known as Old Hale Way was also once called Ickleford Road.

Cambridge Road as it crosses the Purwell in Walsworth early in the twentieth century. The cottages on both sides of the road are gone now, but fruit trees from the gardens still bear plums in season. When electricity was installed in the cottages on the left in 1945, the inhabitants found their homes noticeably colder than they had been with gas lighting. At the centre of the picture is Walsworth House, now part of North Hertfordshire College. A bomb damaged the bridge during the Second World War, and traffic was restricted whilst repairs were affected. In the early nineteenth century there was only a ford crossing at this point.

Walsworth Road at the junction with Whinbush Road, c. 1905. This is a view that has changed very little in almost 100 years. The lodge on the corner was thatched; it is now roofed with Canadian cedar shingles. It once formed part of the Hermitage estate. A tunnel runs beneath Walsworth Road in this area, connecting what was once the garden of the Hermitage with Rawlings Dell. On the right stands St Luke's Home of Rest for the Sick and Infirm, run by a Miss Thackthwaite. Hitchin residents paid 7s a week to recuperate from illness there.

Five

Demolition

The Croft during its demolition in 1964/65. The age of the building was not enough to save it. This view is from the garden, once a showpiece of Victorian horticulture. There were formal beds, lawns and a fernery.

During demolition of the Croft, this fine crown post came to light in the roof space. It was made of substantial timbers, held together with wooden pegs called treenails. The posts carried much of the weight of the roof. The lath and plaster partitions are a later addition.

The Croft had a well in its cellar. It was filled with rubble, and difficult to date. It was almost certainly older than the town piped water supply of around 1850: a building of the status of the Croft would have been one of the early subscribers to the new service.

The Lairage Poultry Auction, which stood between Paynes Park and Old Park Road, now the site of Safeway and the multi-storey car park. Trading in poultry and rabbits continued here until the 1970s. The Poultry Auction was the last of Hitchin's livestock markets to go.

Brand Street, the site for Sainsbury's supermarket, which has since moved to the area between Bancroft and Whinbush Road. Several buildings were knocked down: the 1904 post office, the Methodist chapel and the Dog public house, dating from at least 1846, once filled this rather forlorn gap.

St Michael's College, Grove Road, in 1971. The original Catholic school moved from Mont Saint-Michel in France in 1903 as a result of anti-clerical laws there. In 1968 the school moved to Stevenage, and the Hitchin buildings were demolished. Roofers can be seen salvaging the slates. The school is remembered in the name of College Close, upon which stands the police station that took its place.

The barn that stood behind Coopers' Arms in Tilehouse Street, during demolition, c. 1980. At first sight this picture is confusing, but in fact it contains a wealth of interesting detail. The main timbers are clearly old, as is some of the brickwork. The straight supports and battens show that the barn has been re-roofed in the not too-distant past, and there are also modern reinforcing cross-timbers.

Opposite below: R. Gunner's butchers shop on the corner of Bancroft and Portmill Lane, c. 1980. Meat hooks hang from the beam in the butchers, which looks unlikely to pass modern hygiene regulations. Next door was the Crown and Lion, visible to the left. The Crown and the White Lion had been demolished to build the new pub, which has now in its turn fallen, in this case to make space for W.H. Smith in 1979.

Bowman's Station Mill during its demolition in 1985. The site had run out of space, despite the purchase and clearing of an adjacent pub for expansion. Production moved to Ickleford, where there was more scope for growth, and Station Mill came down. The site is now occupied by a DIY store.

Six

Events

Hitchin Early Closing Association rally, 1897. The spread of gas lighting led to increasingly late opening hours for shops, and the Early Closing Association was a reaction in support of shop workers. In Hitchin the association was supported by local politicians, clergy and other prominent citizens, and from 1 July 1850 many shops in the town closed as early as 8 p.m., Saturdays excepted.

The premises of Ellis & Everard Ltd at No. 30 Bancroft. The company was established in 1848; their head office was in Leicester. They traded as 'coal, coke, salt, English and foreign timber and general builders' merchants'. This photograph shows the decorations put up for Queen Victoria's Diamond Jubilee in 1897.

The south side of the Market Place, again during Queen Victoria's Diamond Jubilee in 1897. Not content with a few flags, Whaley's Haircutting Rooms have gone to town with a portrait of the Queen, surrounded by foliage. The shutters are up on all the premises, so this photograph was probably taken on the jubilee day itself.

The opening of the new town hall in Brand Street in 1901. The fire brigade and the Yeomanry bicycle troop are both present. The cycles are fitted with brackets to carry the soldiers' rifles.

The Coronation of Edward VII in 1902. This float was referred to as the 'Empire Car' and was entered by the Hitchin Conservative Working Men's Club. Different nations of the British Empire are represented, including Wales, Newfoundland, Egypt, West Africa and New Zealand. Whether one approves of empire or not, it is clear that a great deal of time and effort went into this remarkable display.

The Coronation of George V pageant, 22 June 1911. The procession passes through the Market Place.

The Coronation pageant of 1911; the procession enters Bancroft. Brand Street and the High Street are to the left of the picture. W.B. Moss & Sons' premises are on the right, with spectators seated on the balcony. The astonishing float in the foreground is once again the entry of the Hitchin Conservative Working Men's Club, built by Barker's timber merchants, and represents the Norman Conquest. Behind them is Kershaw's coach, last heard of in the 1950s when it was sold to a film company. It is believed to be on one of the Mediterranean islands.

Opposite below: The Coronation of Queen Elizabeth II, 1953: a thatched cottage in Wymondley Road. It was not just the town centre that was decorated on royal occasions; some of the humbler dwellings on the outskirts received similar treatment. This is the same cottage shown in an earlier picture, and was taken not long before its demolition.

More of the procession passes further down Bancroft. The building on the right is A. Waters, household furnisher. Two doors up is the police station, completed in 1885. The interest amongst the pedestrians seems to have waned.

The dedication of the war memorial by Lord Hampden in the churchyard after the First World War. The names of those killed in the Second World War have been added to the monument.

Seven

Leisure

The Queen Street swimming pool. Doris, Beatie and Ruby Howard pose in the pool in June 1928. The changing rooms are behind the three girls. The site of the pool is now covered by Jill Grey Place.

The Queen Street pool from the exterior. The pool was of course unheated, and it could be pretty cold. The water came from the Hiz, and was changed once a week. By the time its week was up it had changed colour, particularly in warm weather.

The Queen Street pool: Bill Abbiss executes a fine swallow dive on a fine summer's day. The spectators' dress dates this picture to the first quarter of the twentieth century.

The new outdoor swimming pool on Butts Close was opened in 1938. It featured a toddlers' pool and diving boards set at one, three and five metres, now removed for reasons of safety. This photograph was taken in 1939 at Hitchin Boys' Grammar School swimming sports day. The water was treated with chlorine but, like the Queen Street pool, it could become pretty murky on a hot weekend.

In the late 1980s the decision was taken to build a new indoor pool in Hitchin, and part of the sunbathing grassland on the Butts Close site was selected as the location. In this view from 1989 excavations are well underway. The trees in the background flank Elmside Walk.

Windmill Hill, which was once owned by Frederic Seebohm; his daughters donated much of it to the town in 1921. This photograph was probably taken a few years before then; the hill was already popular for walks and for picnicking. Rawlings Dell is behind the fence to the right; during the Second World War it was a practice range for the Home Guard. Cartridge cases and even hand grenades were found there by adventurous post-war schoolboys. The gardens on both sides of Hermitage Road were part of the Hermitage estate.

Bancroft Recreation Ground in the early 1960s. The Recreation Ground occupies land that was once osier beds, where willows were grown in the damp soil for the production of the raw material for the town's basket makers. The land was purchased by Hitchin Urban District Council in 1924 and transformed into pleasant gardens, with tennis courts and a small pool suitable for paddling and model boats. The pool has been filled in now, because of the dangers of broken glass to children's feet. There were also putting and bowling greens.

The south side of Butts Close, around 1890, with a travelling fair, though it seems to be a small-scale affair. The gallopers furthest from the camera are steam powered – the chimney can be seen projecting from the canopy. Butts Close remains the venue for funfairs today, though the nature of many of the attractions has changed. Steam has long since given way to petrol and diesel generators.

Butts Close, looking south, on a fine summer's evening in 1954. The trees that surround the close are established, but still quite small; they were planted in 1937 to commemorate the Coronation of George VI, following the abdication of his brother, Edward VIII. Bedford Road is to the right of the picture.

Oughtonhead Common, *c.* 1901. With its attractive riverside, the common is still popular with walkers. This early view of the waterfall, the run-off from Westmill millpond, is less common than the one most often seen. Before water abstraction reduced the flow of the river, the Oughton was much deeper, and Reginald Hine was able to write in 1935 that the Oughton 'contains many trout, some of a considerable size'. Regrettably no longer.

Ickleford Road, and Blake Bros' Picturedrome, built by William and Ernie Blake in 1910/11. They showed films as well as staging music hall and circus acts. Though it is not possible to be certain, the decorations make it likely that this picture was taken in June 1911, at the time of George V's Coronation. The building displays its original frontage, with a separate door on the left labelled 'Pit Entrance Admission'.

Blake's Picturedrome in its new, more imposing, incarnation. The new frontage was built in 1916, which ties in nicely with the poster on the side wall advertising *Tom Brown's Schooldays*. Made that year, it was the first film to be given a Royal Command Performance, for King George V and Queen Mary at Buckingham Palace on 24 February 1917. The building remains standing, though in the 1960s it was much altered.

The Regal Cinema in Bancroft opened in 1939. It closed its doors thirty-eight years later, in 1977. For a while it seemed that this remarkable building might be saved, but though it reopened in 1980 after conversion to a concert hall and recording studio, it was too good to last. A doctors' surgery called Regal Chambers now occupies the site. This picture was taken in 1978, after the ground floor windows had been boarded up.

The Hermitage Cinema stood in Hermitage Road. In this 1951 view the cinema stands on the right, next to Barker's Yard. The Hermitage had a stage, dressing rooms and an orchestra pit. Built in the 1930s, it closed its doors in 1963. The quantity of motor traffic in this picture is unusual for the time.

This picture, taken from a town directory, depicts the Hertfordshire Hounds Christmastide meet on Boxing Day 1954 in Hitchin Market Place. In the days before political correctness and a different attitude toward animals, the Hunt was a colourful spectacle that drew large crowds.

Eight

The Fire Brigade

Hitchin fire brigade in 1887, with its new Shand-Mason horse-drawn steam engine in Priory Park. The previous engine had been hand pumped, so the new machine was a dramatic step forward in fire-fighting technology. Nonetheless, it was still drawn by horses, and could take some time to reach any fire in outlying districts. It was christened 'St George' by its operators.

Grove Mill in Grove Road, 1889. Hitchin fire brigade was already long established when the mill caught fire. The building, erected in 1814, is on an ancient milling site once known as Burnt Mill in commemoration of an earlier disaster. Overheated bearings were thought to be the cause of the blaze. Though the mill seems to be beyond repair, in fact it still exists, though the top floor was demolished. Its survival may in part be due to the immense thickness of the walls.

In 1916 a Mercedes tractor vehicle replaced the horses as the means of getting to fires. Two years later, the Shand-Mason engine failed its boiler test and was replaced by a similar pump. This picture was taken in Sun Street in 1921 and shows the Mercedes in use at the funeral of chief fire officer C.L. Barham. He had served in the brigade for fifty of his sixty-eight years.

In 1923 a new engine was ordered for the brigade, a motorized Morris Guy. It was not their first choice – they would have preferred a Merryweather, but it was too expensive. The Morris Guy, seen here in 1926, could only pump 150-250 gallons of water per minute, but it only cost £800.

An unofficial use for the fire engine: on 12 September 1927, fireman Abbiss, who had served since 1 February 1924, married Miss Day at St Mary's church. His colleagues crossed axes as the couple walked from the church, and they were taken home on the decorated engine. The decorative ironwork of the church gates is visible to each side of the vehicle.

The Shand-Mason engine had not been consigned to the scrap heap however. It continued in service as a supplementary machine, as this photograph from 1927 shows. The engine is under pressure, and beneath it is a pile of ash from its fire.

The brigade covered the villages as well as Hitchin town. In this picture, taken on 22 December 1927, the White Horse garage at Pirton is on fire. When the proprietor, Mr P.H. Wright, was testing the 'Pirton Belle' motor bus it backfired, setting light to the premises. He managed to save the bus, but by the time the brigade arrived it was too late for the garage – the lucky horseshoe on the pillar at the centre of the picture apparently failed to work. The petrol pump on the right indicates a potentially explosive situation.

On Wednesday 9 November 1927, the brigade was called to fight a haystack fire at Langley End. It was a bitterly cold night, and ice formed on the hosepipes as they pumped water onto the ricks. Unfortunately the pond they were pumping from ran dry after two hours, and all they could do was pull the stacks apart and let them burn out. The only bright spot of the evening was the baking of potatoes in the fire!

29 February 1928, and a burning lorry in Walsworth Road. The four-ton 'Saurer' was passing the memorial gateway to the Caldicott School when the driver was warned his vehicle was on fire. The local newspaper reported that the flames made 'a thrilling spectacle', and noted that the damage, which cost an estimated £80, was not covered by insurance. Fortunately the petrol tank did not explode.

This shed and car in Lancaster Avenue were completely destroyed on 15 February 1929. The brigade was called out at 12.15 p.m., but there was nothing they could do, and they were back at the fire station an hour later. The fire must have been intense: the tyres on the car and the paint from the number plate have completely disappeared.

A Hitchin postcard showing several views, postmarked 1917 and sent by Charles Loftus Barham to Gunner Herbert Barham at North Everington War Hospital, Leicester, where he was recuperating after being wounded during the First World War. The scenes include the High Street, the Market Place, the Sailor Boy and, rather oddly, 'The Avenue, Stevenage'. The round pictures are of the Corn Exchange, unidentified thatched cottages, and the entrance to Chapman's Yard.

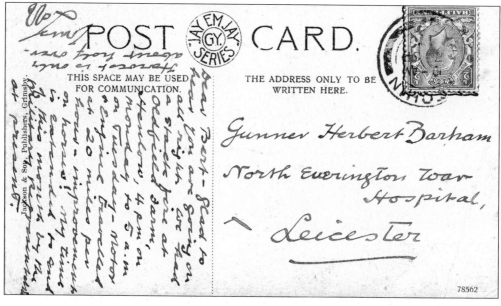

The reverse of the previous postcard. Loftus Barham was chief fire officer, and Herbert had served with him before joining the forces. The text reads, in part, 'Dear Bert, Glad to hear you are going on all right. We had a stack fire at Oldfield Farm, Henlow, 4 p.m. on Monday to 5 a.m. on Tuesday – Motor and Engine travelled at 20 miles per hour – improvement on horses!' Once a fireman, it would seem, always a fireman.

Nine
Snow

Hermitage Road from Windmill Hill on a snowy winter's day, c. 1880. Though many early photographs were of good quality, some, like this one, fell short of the mark. The number of mature trees in this area was once considerable, and is particularly striking in this picture.

St Mary's church from the south east during the winter of 1962/63. Those old enough to remember that year will not easily forget it. Snow piled up on Butts Close for weeks on end, until even the children got sick of it.

St Mary's church from the north east on 6 January 1985. The river is frozen over.

The south-west entrance to the churchyard, January 1985. At that time Halseys extended to the end of the buildings on the right.

The Dower House at the junction of Stevenage Road and London Road, 10 January 1953. A dower house was a building set aside for a widow from her husband's estate, but this building is far too late for that. It is said however that during demolition in 1986 the remnants of an earlier structure were discovered within the fabric of the building, but too late to be saved. Dower Court, a block of flats, now covers the site.

Deep snow in Bridge Street, probably 1962/63. The pub sign on the right is the King's Head. The original pub of that name was in Queen Street, and was demolished in 1961; the name was transferred to the Plough in Bridge Street.

If Windmill Hill was popular for walking and picnicking in summer, it was equally popular for tobogganing in winter. A considerable speed could be achieved on its steep slopes, but sledgers had to be careful of both the road at the bottom and the sheer drop into Hollow Lane on the south side. This picture was taken in the winter of 1940/41.

The top of Tilehouse Street, 1959. Before the Priory bypass, Tilehouse Street was the main route from Stevenage to Luton and Bedford. Heavy lorries shook the old buildings, and this was a major consideration in the new road scheme. This view is now blocked. In the background is the Waggon and Horses, almost obscured by the snow.

A cold day in Bancroft in the early twentieth century. The building second from the left is Woodlands, once the home of Quaker banker Joseph Sharples. In 1871 it became a school for boys, and later the grammar school. Originally both girls and boys occupied the same site, until a new school on Windmill Hill was built for the girls in 1908.

Another bleak winter in Bancroft, this time in 1962/63 and looking south to Moss's Corner. It is little surprise that the two men on foot constitute the only traffic. The weight of the snow has brought down branches on the right.

Ten
Schools and Churches

Walsworth school in Woolgrove Road, 1915. The teacher is Miss Gurney. The school was founded by Mary Exton, née Ransom, and opened in 1852 with nineteen children. School hours were 9 a.m. to 4 p.m. with two hours for lunch. The school logbooks record numerous absences, and many of the excuses reflect the rural nature of Walsworth: 'gleaning', 'taking meals to parents in the field' and 'blackberry picking'.

St Michael's College in its early years, probably around 1910. The Catholic Edmundian fathers brought the school from Brittany to Hitchin in 1903 and the buildings were ready for occupation in 1906. In an effort to make the school as English as they could, they appointed an English headmaster.

Hitchin Boys' Grammar School, the South Court, c. 1920. The building on the left was the masters' boarding house, and when built in 1901 it housed the headmaster, the teachers and the boys who boarded at the school. The section with the cupola was originally the school hall, but later became the library; to the right of the entrance was, when the present author attended the school in the 1960s, the worst part of all – the headmaster's office.

Hitchin Boys' Grammar School, 1903. Mr Abbiss and boys exercising in the gymnasium of the Blue Cross Temperance Brigade, now part of the town hall. Before he became a member of staff, Mr Abbiss was paid an annual fee for his tuition.

Hitchin Boys' Grammar School, the North Court, July 1943. The inspection of 7th Hertfordshire (Hitchin) Company Army Cadet Force by F. Parker and Col. E. Phillips. The boys' rifles are Rifle No. 3s, made in the USA in .303 calibre during the First World War and sold to Britain at that time.

St Faith's church in Woolgrove Road was built in the nineteenth century as an off-shoot of St Saviour's. The cottages on the right appear on maps as early as 1766. They were demolished in 1969. The noticeboard to the right advertises that Hitchin Town Football Club are due to play Bromley.

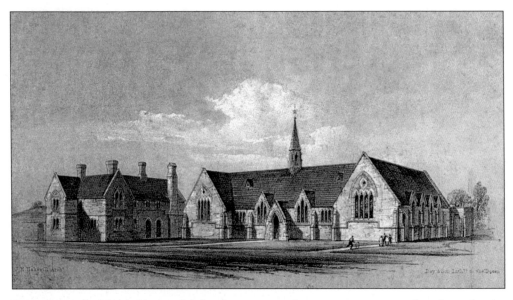

Biggin Lane, St Mary's National School: a nineteenth-century engraving, thought to be the architect's impression, *c.* 1851. The building appears to be of stone rather than the brick eventually used, and the figures seem remarkably small, even for children. These may have been deliberate ploys by the architect to make the building seem imposing and attractive to the customer, or brick might have been chosen as a cheaper option than stone.

Biggin Lane, St Mary's school – the reality. Built in 1854, the school is very similar in design to the previous illustration. The brick patterning is nicely done. The building came down in around 1970 to make way for the market, which at the time was held in St Mary's Square.

Nightingale Road, the Roman Catholic Church. Though the plot was purchased in 1899, the church was not built until 1902. This view must be later than 1907, because it was in that year that the bell tower was added. The ornate combined horse trough and gas lamp is a particularly fine example, and perhaps served as an unofficial roundabout.

St Mary's church from the south, a night scene from 1984. For many years the church has been floodlit at night, which, as this picture shows, can be a very dramatic sight. The site as a place of worship is said to date back to the eighth century, but the earliest recognizable part of the structure is Norman. Most of the church dates from between the thirteenth and fifteenth centuries.

Eleven

Public Houses

The Coopers' Arms, Tilehouse Street, an early engraving. The building dates from the fifteenth century and was once more extensive than it is today. According to local tradition, a tunnel runs from the cellars to the Priory, though its purpose is unexplained; on the whole, it seems most unlikely. In this view the stone mullions of the windows are still in place. The small building to the left has now gone to provide access to the car park.

The Coopers' Arms, Tilehouse Street, late nineteenth century. John Webb, the licensee, is known to have been landlord in the 1880s. His billboard advertises horses, carriages, traps and good stabling. The windows have been altered to their present form.

The Red Cow in the Market Place, in the 1960s. The building dates from the seventeenth century, and has an interesting cellar that projects for some distance into the Market Place, as do several other premises in the area. The pub has closed, but the building remains. The first record of its use as an inn dates from 1731.

The Red Lion, Bucklersbury, *c.* 1890. The pub was taken over by McMullen's and rebuilt in about 1904. On the left is Ernest Leete's shop as it used to be; the frontage was refurbished before 1899. The Red Lion is a pub no more, but its 1904 lion still projects from above the ground floor. It is, however, no longer red!

The Royal Oak, Bridge Street, was formerly known as the Boot. Its name was changed in the 1890s. The *Household Almanack* [sic] for 1899, published by Paternoster & Hales, lists the innkeeper in that year as Mr A. Hitchens. This picture probably dates from about that time. The building still stands, though the cement render has been removed, revealing the timber frame beneath.

The Three Tuns in Tilehouse Street. Local tradition had it that the landlord would not serve you if you stumbled on the step. If you stumbled as you left, it was not his problem. The pub belonged to Messrs J.W. Green, 'Noted Luton Ales', who were taken over by Simpsons, who in turn became part of the Whitbread Group. The pub later became Harding's Newsagents.

The Three Tuns, Tilehouse Street, in poor condition in the 1970s. It has since been renovated and returned to its former glory, though as a private house. The building's history is remembered in the house name, 'The Old Three Tuns'.

The Red Hart, Bucklersbury, around 1930, the yard and stables are on the left. Little has changed in this part of the Red Hart yard, though the interior of the pub has been altered. Though the Coopers Arms is an older building, the Red Hart is probably the oldest inn in Hitchin, dating from the second half of the sixteenth century.

The Highlander, Upper Tilehouse Street, *c.* 1898. The building is listed as '17th century, altered'. It was reputedly a drovers' pub, originally frequented by men who brought cattle to the market. Amongst the bills posted on the building on the right are advertisements for *Amateur Gardening* magazine and Sandy Flower Show. To the right of centre is the junction of the roads to Luton and Pirton.

The Waggon & Horses, on the corner of Old Park Road and Tilehouse Street, in about 1970. Next door is Ashwell's General Stores. The site is now occupied by the county court. The Waggon & Horses opened its doors as a pub in 1842 and fell to progress 130 years later.

The Orange Tree, Stevenage Road, as it used to be. This pub has been rebuilt twice – first in 1927, and again in 1977, when the building shown here was completely demolished. The left front of the pub was an off-licence, a not uncommon feature of pubs at the time; the Ship in Walsworth had a similar facility.

The Angel Vaults in Sun Street, not long before its demolition in 1958. The building dated from 1450, though it is said that part of it was destroyed by fire when Henry VIII was staying there in 1523. The King escaped, but with 'not so much a shirt upon his back'. For many years the inn hosted the ecclesiastical court of the Archdeacon of Huntingdon. In the nineteenth century the building was rendered with cement to give an impression of stonework. The decoration in this picture is a later addition.

The Cock Inn, High Street, c. 1890. Though the original building dates from between the fifteenth and sixteenth centuries, it has been much altered. Everything up to and including the second gable from the left was knocked down for Woolworth's '3d and 6d Stores' in the 1930s. The three-storey section that exists today to the right of the third gable was built for the landlord Alfred Doughty, who ran the pub for almost thirty years until his death in 1916.

The Dog, Brand Street, c. 1960. At that time the pub sign depicted a black spaniel, but it was not always so – in 1939 the sign was a silhouette of a dog of an indeterminate breed. The pub, along with other buildings, was demolished to make way for Sainsbury's supermarket. Next door is Saunders' garage. Behind the Jaguar can be seen the petrol pumps. To avoid blocking the pavement the pipes swung out over pedestrians' heads on supports.

Opposite below: The Crown and the White Lion, in Bancroft were knocked down in the late 1960s. A new pub, the Crown and Lion, was built on part of the site. Its most unusual feature was the 'Dive Bar', below ground level. The pub did not last long, and was in turn demolished; W.H. Smith now stands on the site. The shop on the left at the corner of Portmill Lane is R. Gunner's butchers shop.

The Troopers' Arms, Bancroft, in 1860. This is one of the best-known photographs of Hitchin, but it is quite irresistible. How old the building was when W.B. Moss knocked it down is not clear. It was rendered, so its timber frame is not visible. A conservative estimate would be in the seventeenth century. On the left is the White Lion and on the right the Three Horseshoes. When this picture was taken the cattle market was held in Bancroft, so the landlord of the time, John Carter, must have done a roaring trade on Tuesdays.

The Old George in Ickleford, seen from the lych-gate of St Katherine's church. The pub is old – there have been suggestions of a twelfth-century date for parts of the structure, and claims that in the thirteenth century it was the site of a leper colony. Most of what we see today probably dates from the fifteenth and sixteenth centuries. The entrance to the lounge bar, on the right, was in 1908 a bay window, and since this picture was taken it has been restored to that function. Otherwise little has changed.

The Old George in Ickleford: the public bar. This magnificent 16ft table ran almost the full length of the bar. Sitting on the far side could be tricky on a busy evening – everyone had to move if you wanted to get out. The owners decided it was being ruined by spilt beer, so they decided to remove it, but they had to take the window out to do so.

Twelve
The Market

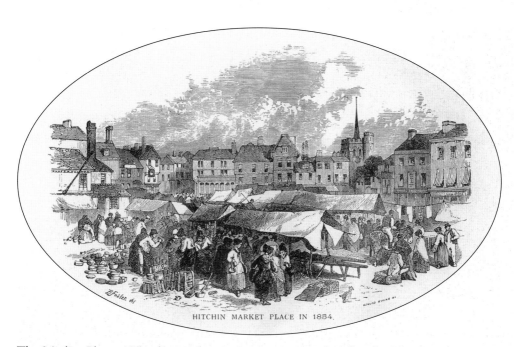

HITCHIN MARKET PLACE IN 1854.

The Market Place, 1854, from an engraving in an 1899 handbook of Hitchin. Insofar as it can be checked, this view is accurate. The buildings on the left are the Shambles, which stood in the west side of Market Place until they were demolished shortly after the date of this picture. Large quantities of straw plait for the Luton hat industry were sold at the market, each length representing considerable investment of time and effort for housewives and young girls in the region.

The Market Place in about 1918. Next to the Corn Exchange is the Playhouse cinema, which boasted 'perfect pictures, refined variety.' It opened in 1913 and closed in 1937. It held seating for 750 people in the stalls and balcony. It even had two private boxes. The interior was lavishly decorated.

Hitchin Market, from a postcard mailed on 31 December 1903. This view shows nicely the alignment of the stalls. Traffic flowed directly from the High Street to Sun Street (and vice versa), and the market layout reflected the traffic pattern. This did not change until after the Second World War. The circular advertisement in the lower left corner reads, 'W. Whaley's Hair Cutting and Shampooing Rooms. Hot, cold and tepid baths. Market Square Hitchin'.

Market day in the early twentieth century, and James Rennie's bookstall. Rennie was born in Australia and raised in Scotland. His stall sold bibles and religious tracts. Later, the Baptist and Foreign Bible Society provided him with a handcart. The posters refer to the Herts and Beds Colportage Society and the *Christian Herald*. Rennie is the bearded man on the right.

Bancroft livestock market, late nineteenth century. In this view, W.B. Moss has yet to demolish the Trooper Inn, which means the photograph was taken in 1899 or earlier. The sun is low, but is shining from close to the south, hence this photograph was taken in the winter. In January 1904, following years of indecision, the market was transferred to Paynes Park, after an unfortunate incident when a child was tossed in the air by a frightened cow.

Cattle in Bancroft on market day. This picture was taken after 1875 – because Hermitage Road can be seen on the right – and before the cattle market was transferred to Paynes Park – because the card is inscribed, 'this is just opposite our school. Eva.' It is possible, however, that the cattle are merely being driven along Bancroft to or from market. If that is the case, the latest date is 1908, when the girls' grammar school moved to Windmill Hill.

Bridge Street, c. 1900. On market day animals came into and went out of the town from all directions. In this case the animals are sheep and cattle in Bridge Street. Today the building on the left displays some interesting bargeboards and door fittings depicting crocodiles, about which there is some confusion. The door ornaments do not appear in this photograph, so they must be additions. Paternoster & Hales' *Hitchin Handbook* of 1899 refers to 'the house with the crocodile gable, by the river in Bridge Street', so the bargeboards are at least as old as that.

Thirteen
Hitchin Miscellany

Hitchin station and goods yards from the air, c. 1920. Hitchin was an important junction. Bottom right is the station, with its canopy. The yards and warehouses of the Great Northern and Midland Railways are centre left. The lines run from London (bottom right) to Peterborough and the north (top left) and Cambridge (top right). The gasworks (centre, top), a source of much pollution, are gone now. Bowman's Mill is visible at the junction of Nightingale and Walsworth Roads.

The town centre from the south in 1929. The medieval layout of the town, from Tilehouse Street (bottom left) to Bancroft (top right), is clearly visible. It was created by infill – temporary market stalls became permanent buildings. A similar pattern can be found in other market towns. Many of the shops have awnings, a feature more common then than now.

The town centre from the south west in the late 1950s. Though there is little obvious change, the omens are there. The Angel Vaults has gone. Cars are parked in the Market Place, St Mary's Square and in Portmill Lane, where buildings have been demolished to make way for them.

A view of Hitchin from Windmill Hill, c. 1905. Centre right is St Mary's church. The area between the camera and the church is now occupied by Garrison Court and Woodcote House. To the left are the slums of the Queen Street area, partially obscured by smoke from their chimneys.

Woolgrove Road, Walsworth. Miss Lily Gibbs ran a small shop from her parlour in the house to the right of the Sailor Boy. The geese belonged to householders in Orchard Road, and were allowed to walk down to the river for a swim; at the same time each day they would leave the river to walk home. Miss Gibbs shut up shop in the 1940s and went to live with her sister in Australia.

Opposite below: Redcoats was the site of one of the more bizarre local episodes. James Lucas, who was born in 1813, became a paranoid recluse in 1849. He turned his home, Elmwood, into a fortress, and restricted his contact with the outside world to a few trusted friends. For twenty-five years he lived in filth and squalor until his death in 1874. This photograph dates from about 1870, and shows Elmwood with its barred windows. The man leaning on the post is believed to be Robert Devine, one of Lucas's bodyguards. The house was pulled down in 1893.

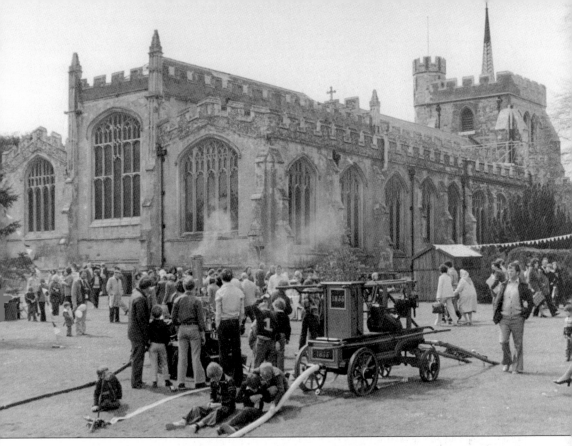

St Mary's Church fête, *c.* 1980. In the foreground are two early fire engines belonging to Derek Wheeler. The Merryweather Manual machine on the right dates from at least 1855. It was common practice to pay men in both money and beer to work these machines. With the coming of steam, the men were no longer required, and there was a noticeable fall in the number of minor fires. The engine on the left is a much later steam-driven Merryweather Valiant.

A First World War food queue in the Market Place. It ran into the churchyard and beyond. Food shortages in the latter part of the war were severe. In this case the police and special constables had to be called out to control the crowd.

Butts Close, c. 1930. After the First World War, trophies were presented to towns throughout the country. Hitchin got two – a tank claimed to be 'Fearless,' an armoured vehicle with an illustrious record, and a German howitzer. In fact, there is reason to believe that the tank was a fraud, as the one presented was not the same model as the real 'Fearless'.

The R101 flies over Hitchin during her trials in 1930. The huge airship and her companion the R100 were housed at Cardington, Bedfordshire. On her last flight the R101 flew over the town on 4 October 1930, before she crashed in France early the following morning, killing all but eight of the fifty-four people aboard. The crash meant the death of the airship industry in Britain, though the enormous hangers still stand.

Butts Close, c. 1930. The First World War relics rapidly became popular, especially with the young. Small boys climbed all over them. In this picture, Mr Frank Wells poses with his grandson, Peter in 1933. The weapon is the German 21cm howitzer. The small girl disappearing to the left is Pansy Wells!

123

Walsworth Home Guard in 1941, outside Grove House, which stood in extensive grounds leading down to the Hiz, on the corner of Grove Road and Cadwell Lane. There are sixty-five officers and men, a pretty good turnout for a village the size of Walsworth. Contrary to the 'Dad's Army' image, very few of the men seem to be elderly. The commanding officer was Lieutenant William Harkness. Corporal W. Scott, front row, far right, only had one leg.

Orchard Road, 6 August 1941. Miriam Simms, née Pepper, was killed by a German bomb. She was pregnant at the time. She is buried in the cemetery off St Johns Road. Miriam is believed to have been the only person killed by direct enemy action in Hitchin. It is still possible to make out shrapnel marks on the buildings on the opposite side of the road.

Fourteen

The Villages

Charlton in the 1940s, from Brick Kiln Lane. The Windmill public house is on the left. Charlton lies on the River Hiz, close to its source at Wellhead, which was the source of Hitchin's first piped water supply in the mid-nineteenth century. Water from wells and from the river in Hitchin was often polluted, and typhoid fever and cholera were common. Charlton is best known as the birthplace, in 1813, of Sir Henry Bessemer, inventor of the blast furnace.

Ickleford, the smithy and green in around 1900. The sign just right of centre is for the Old George pub. The lych-gate leads to St Katherine's church, parts of which date from the twelfth century. Local tradition has it that a tunnel runs between the two buildings, but the evidence is scanty. The pub to the left is the Green Man, since demolished and rebuilt. The smithy is now a newsagents' shop. Just off this picture, to the right, on the green, stood a street lamp erected in commemoration of Queen Victoria's Diamond Jubilee in 1897.

Ickleford Common was grazed until the late 1980s. Unusually, it remained unploughed during the Second World War, and has retained its diversity of plant species. The common encloses almost twenty-two hectares. The date of this picture is difficult to estimate, as very little has changed over the years; it could be any time between 1900 and 1950.

Ickleford Manor was a most unlucky building. The Georgian manor caught fire in November 1919, just as extensive alterations and redecorations were being completed. The fire brigade worked for nine hours to try and contain the flames, with little success. The manor was rebuilt, only to catch fire again in 1953. This photograph was taken during the later fire.

Walsworth, c. 1920. The River Purwell opposite the Sailor Boy was an extremely popular vantage point for photographers. This picture, taken from much closer to Walsworth crossroads, is unusual. Much of this view remains unchanged today.

THE CAGE STOTFOLD.

Stotfold, the village lockup in the early twentieth century. Stotfold is really outside the scope of this book, but I could not resist this picture. The lock-up was used in most instances for drunks, though more serious offenders might be incarcerated in it on a temporary basis, pending transfer to a more secure establishment. The structure appears in a state of disrepair, its right-hand side being used for the posting of bills. Such small cells were once common; several still stand in Hertfordshire.

Henlow Aerodrome, c. 1925, about five miles from Hitchin. The aircraft in front of the hanger is a Bristol Fighter F2B in post-war colours. Behind the 'Brisfit' are two de Havilland DH9s; the other aircraft in the picture remain unidentified. The F2B and DH9 were both two-seaters, and entered service in 1917. RAF Henlow opened in 1918 as an aircraft depot. Many of the airmen from Henlow were housed in Hitchin; parts of Heathfield Road were built especially for them.